I'm a Princess

Written by Kirsten Hall

Illustrated by Dee deRosa

children's press ®

A Division of Scholastic Inc.

New York Toronto London Auckland Sydney
Mexico City New Delhi Hong Kong
Danbury, Connecticut

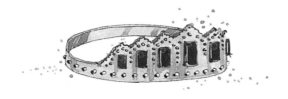

Library of Congress Cataloging-in-Publication Data

Hall, Kirsten.
  I'm a princess / written by Kirsten Hall ; illustrated by Dee
deRosa.– [1st American ed.].
        p. cm. – (My first reader)
Summary: Dressed as a princess, a girl expects her family to treat her
royally, but that is because Halloween has arrived.
  ISBN 0-516-22928-1 (lib. bdg.)   0-516-24630-5 (pbk.)
  [1. Princesses–Fiction. 2. Halloween–Fiction. 3. Stories in rhyme.]
I. DeRosa, Dee, ill. II. Title. III. Series.
  PZ8.3.H146Iaah 2003
  [E]–dc21
                                  2003003633

Text © 1995 Nancy Hall, Inc.
Illustrations © 1995 Dee deRosa
Published in 2003 by Children's Press
A Division of Scholastic Inc.

1 2 3 4 5 6 7 8 9 10 R 12 11 10 09 08 07 06 05 04 03

Note to Parents and Teachers

Once a reader can recognize and identify the 30 words
used to tell this story, he or she will be able to read successfully
the entire book. These 30 words are repeated throughout the story,
so that young readers will be able to easily recognize the words
and understand their meaning.

The 30 words used in this book are:

a	is	see
are	it	shoe
bed	make	tells
care	me	the
clothes	my	tie
do	nails	to
don't	no	true
hair	one	wear
I	pretty	what
I'm	princess	you

I'm a princess.

5

It is true.

Make my bed!

Tie my shoe!

No one tells me what to do!

14

No one tells me what to wear!

I'm a princess! I don't care!

See my nails?

20

See my hair?

See the pretty clothes I wear?

23

I'm a princess.

It is true.

I'm a princess.

What are you?

ABOUT THE AUTHOR

Kirsten Hall has lived most of her life in New York City. While she was still in high school, she published her first book for children, *Bunny, Bunny*. Since then, she has written and published more than sixty children's books. A former early education teacher, Kirsten currently works as a children's book editor.

ABOUT THE ILLUSTRATOR

Dee deRosa loves to draw and paint, especially for children's books. She has illustrated more than forty books and each one is her favorite while she is working on it. DeRosa lives in upstate New York in a very rural area where there is lots of snow for skiing in the winter and lots of trails for horseback riding in the summer.